AF898467

FREE YOURSELF TO WORK ON YOUR BUSINESS

HOW UNIT ECONOMICS DRIVES **STRONG LEADERSHIP AND DECISION MAKING**

FREE YOURSELF TO WORK ON YOUR BUSINESS

HOW UNIT ECONOMICS DRIVES ***STRONG LEADERSHIP AND DECISION MAKING***

RUSSELL BENAROYA

Stride Services
www.stride.services

SHEMOTO PRESS

Published by Shemoto Press, Seattle, Washington
www.russellbenaroya.com

Cover design: Moses, Pro_graphics360
Edited and designed by The Writing Desk, LLC
Editorial and interior images: Bailey Lang

ISBN (paperback): 978-1-7370739-3-2
ISBN (eBook): 978-1-7370739-2-5
Library of Congress Control Number: 2021922908

REVIEWS AND PRAISE

As the CEO of a company that provides senior level financial guidance and bookkeeping for venture-stage and growth companies, we know how important it is to empower our clients with information to make better business decisions. We want them equipped to know the right questions to ask. Russell uses an elegantly simple case study to distill complex strategic concepts into specific actions any emerging leader can take to make more informed business decisions and focus time and resources on the things that matter most.

—Chris Fenster
Founder and CEO, Propeller Industries

I'm in the business of helping our clients achieve their highest and best use by leveraging information for better decision making. Russell lays out a very practical set of recommendations for how business leaders can not only ask better questions but also have an understanding where the data originates in the first place. He's not trying to create accountants. He's trying to make smarter business leaders

—Eric Page
Co-founder and CEO, Stride Services

Free Yourself to Work on Your Business is a practical guide for how to get smarter as a business owner on understanding how to make better data driven decisions. Russell lays it out in an easy to understand format that is designed to build confidence but not require me to become a finance wizard. *Free Yourself to Work on Your Business* is perfect for that professional services owner that wants to add an arrow in their quiver of leadership.

—Paige Buck
Partner and Chief Strategy Officer, Kennedy Events

I highly recommend any startup entrepreneur or long-term business operator to embrace the concepts Russell dives into in *Free Yourself to Work On Your Business*. Russell provides practical and useful strategies that you can use immediately to source data, process the data, and ultimately make smarter and better decisions. In this economic environment, unit economics is a key differentiator and essential to building a sustainable and meaningful enterprise.

—Andy Liu
Partner, Unlock Venture Partners

I coach leaders and their teams on how to build and operate high performing sales organizations. Especially at growing organizations, it's important to understand what they are selling and the impact each win has. *Free Yourself to Work on Your Business* is a simple guide for business owners to blend their desire for growth with an understanding of their financial engine.

—Nitya Kirat
CEO, YOSD Consulting and Author of Winning Virtually

DEDICATION

Free Yourself to Work On Your Business *is dedicated to all of my colleagues at Stride Services who spend their days helping business leaders achieve their highest and best use.*

CONTENTS

INTRODUCTION

Entrepreneurs begin with a vision—to develop a better solution to a problem. Entrepreneurs are driven by an internal fire that pushes them to make an impact, to create a legacy, and to build economic success. Entrepreneurs want to create freedom in their lives, the freedom to work on their business, not in their business

If that sounds like you, then you're in the right place.

That was also me. In 2004, I co-founded a healthcare service business called REM Medical, which operated clinics to diagnose and treat sleep disorders. I was excited to be taking the entrepreneurial leap, because our work mattered, and we wanted to help people. But what became very clear, very quickly was that we couldn't help anyone if we didn't have a sound, profitable business model that would keep the doors open.

Keeping our doors open meant we needed to understand the revenue and costs associated with each of our facilities. The machine of the business needed to function in order to make an impact on people's lives—but the machine is not simply being able to account for revenue and expenses.

The machine, in fact, is a deep understanding of **unit economics**. In this short book, I'm going to explain the concept of unit economics, why it is critical for you to understand it, and how it can help you create a business where you are in command of all the levers.

Who Should Read This Book?

If you operate a business that generates revenue on a project or engagement basis, this book is for you. If you run a marketing agency, consulting firm, design firm, engineering firm, or any comparable business, this book is for you. If your business typically manages a lot of engagements at one time, if you have a difficult time seeing into the economics of a project or making course corrections, this book is for you. If you look at your business accounts and simply see that you have more money in the bank this month than you did last month, you might be missing a big opportunity—and this book is for you.

Many businesses struggle with a lack of insight and understanding, leading them to enter into unprofitable engagements, because they can't answer the fundamental questions around pricing and resource allocations needed to create a sustainable business model.

Entrepreneurship is always a risky proposition, whether due to unexpected changes in the market environment or global upheavals like those caused by the covid-19 pandemic. Do you know how your company will manage in a downturn? Many agencies do well when the economy is expanding: they have work, they have customers, the money is coming in. What happens when the economic environment is less certain? Do you know what levers to pull to ensure the doors stay open?

In many cases, we as entrepreneurs wait too long to address the business side of our craft or passion. We readily embrace the creative and visionary outlets that let us pursue our goals but tend to hope that the business side will work out. Atul Gawande, internationally recognized surgeon and CEO of the Bezos/Buffett/Dimon healthcare company Haven says, “Hope is not a plan.” When the economy is chugging along and things are going smoothly, relying on hope alone may work (along with some luck).

When the chips are down, the economy is struggling, and the imperative is that the business fundamentals have to be addressed, many agencies operate from a place of fear and lack of information. They simply don’t have the knowledge of what levers to pull to make fact-based business decisions. This book is intended to provide you with an introduction to some of those levers, through the lens of unit economics.

Getting the Most out of This Book

Understanding unit economics doesn’t require you to become an accountant. In fact, that’s the last thing I want great entrepreneurs to become. Understanding unit economics empowers you to know how to ask the right questions of your control tower, make proactive observations and decisions, and get in control of your business. That’s when you work *on* your business, not *in* it.

Working on your business requires you make a commitment to valuing your time. Too often, business owners spend time on activities that won’t change the trajectory of their organization. I’m going to ask you to value your time at $700 to $900/hour. Whether you explicitly charge that today or not isn’t the point—the point is that how you make decisions about where to spend your time must be in line with the value you, uniquely, can create. Grasping and interpreting the levers of your unit economics will allow you to spend valuable time making decisions, not wasting time trying to figure out how to get information to take action.

Here are some quick reminders that your time is valuable and to check that you are maximizing it.

- You don't have time for projects that will only produce small, incremental results.
- A virtual assistant is worth the money.
- A bookkeeper or CPA is more valuable than keeping track of receipts and QuickBooks and taxes yourself.
- You can't afford to overwork or risk your health by working ineffectively.
- You should be obsessed with doubling your productivity.

You will get the most out of this book when you are committed to working *on* your business. Unit economics will give you the insight that you desire. Unfortunately, unit economics is a concept that eludes too many entrepreneurs. In this book, I will define unit economics, break it down, and use it to answer some really important business questions.

Why Me and Why Stride?

Stride is a national virtual back-office bookkeeping and accounting firm, focused on helping agency owners manage their books and maximize their unit economics. Our purpose at Stride is as follows:

> "We help individuals with a thirst for continuous improvement find their highest and best use, by grounding story with fact. We do that through providing bookkeeping and accounting services."

Grounding story in fact is foundational to business-building. Agencies are masters of storytelling, but sometimes those stories can be deceptive—especially when applied to internal financial performance. It's easy to say, "We wouldn't be in this position if we'd just closed that one deal," or, "We would be more profitable if our account managers just handled the clients better." You might be right, but you might not. At Stride, we help you use fact-based data to ask and answer real questions about the performance of your business.

The machine of any business requires controls and levers. Understanding unit economics will help you develop the flight controls you need to be able to act quickly and make informed decisions. It's not enough to know that your business is ascending or descending. You also need to know your destination and how to get there. When you understand the instrumentation and levers, it will not only breed confidence for you and your team, but for your investors and customers as well.

I co-founded Stride after many years working in finance in Los Angeles and New York and building two healthcare organizations in Seattle. The reason I wanted to start Stride was that I realized that there is so much valuable information that is created in the course of running your business that just gets filed away in financial records that never get used, and that's a real loss.

Imagine if you could harness that information. Imagine if, rather than filing away your history of activity, you actually brought it to life and started using it to make smarter decisions. Yes, the history may not be an indication of future performance, but it certainly informs the path ahead. For me, Stride combined my finance and operating experience into an opportunity to support thousands of entrepreneurs to get and stay in their zone of genius.

1. OVERVIEW OF UNIT ECONOMICS

Let's start with the basics. What is unit economics? **Unit economics** represents the value of the thing that you sell, and the variable costs associated with selling it.

UNIT ECONOMICS:

The revenue of the thing you sell, and the variable costs of selling it

Revenue - variable costs = unit economics

Simple, right? You generate revenue, and you incur some costs in order to generate that revenue, costs that change (are variable) depending on how much revenue you generate. Why am I making such a big deal out of something so simple? Well, because many of us get tripped up when we try to define "unit" and how to capture the costs associated with it. For example, a **unit** can be calculated through the lens of a customer, a service, or a product. Armed with your unit data, you can ask questions like, "How profitable is this customer?" or "How profitable is this project?" or "How profitable is this item to manufacture and sell?"

Unit economics gives you the unfiltered reality about whether you have an intrinsically profitable business. Being "intrinsically profitable" means that you generate more revenue than the variable costs associated with earning that revenue. So theoretically, when the thing you sell and the cost you incur to sell that thing is greater than $1, you have an intrinsically profitable business. You might need to sell a lot of those units to cover the fixed costs (rent, general and administrative costs, other overhead), but it is intrinsically profitable. Congratulations! That is the foundation of business health.

Those of you who have dealt with investors know that any smart investor will challenge you to explain your unit economics. There is a funny (funny as in funny to people like me, I guess) quip in unit economics where someone says, "Well, we lose a little money on every customer, but we make it up in volume." Ha! There is no amount of volume that your business can generate to become profitable if you lose money on every customer.

But here's the thing: There are plenty of businesses that have raised money on a failed unit economics model...they just typically don't last. Not everyone manages to find a book like this one before it's too late.

Let's take the company Bento as an example. Bento was founded in 2015 by Jason Demant and Vincent Cardillo, with $1.5 million in venture capital funding. The service was to provide customizable delivery bento boxes—a genius idea on the surface. But, as Demant told Food on Demand, "Toward the end of 2015 is when we realized that this model we were pursuing was not something that we were able to succeed in just from a unit economics standpoint." By the time the company transitioned away from direct-to-consumer sales to wholesaling, it was too late.

What's the lesson here? You *cannot* scale an unprofitable business. Growth in volume does not make up for losing money on each unit. Study your unit economics and make sure that the unit you are evaluating (customer, product, or service) is profitable. Then, find ways to optimize it.

Unit Types

Take a moment here to think broadly about your own business. What is a unit for your company? The concept of a unit can be broken down into a few different categories.

Unit Type	Customer	Service	Products
Example	Netflix, Terminix, ClassPass	Marketing agencies, consulting firms, event management companies	GoPro, Lululemon, The Gap

Unit as a Customer

This is a common unit definition in recurring revenue businesses (often in technology, you hear the term "SaaS," or "Software as a Service") where your customer continues to buy your service predictably over time. Some well-known companies you certainly know would be Spotify or Netflix. But even non-tech companies like fitness company ClassPass or your local exterminator, Terminix, would be good examples.

Unit as a Service

Marketing and consulting firms sell their services on a project basis. Event management companies work with individuals or groups to host conferences, trainings, seminars, and so on. Units as a Service tend to be discrete, rather than recurring, and have contracted beginning and end dates.

Unit as a Product

Take GoPro, for example. Their unit is the wearable camera. Is that unit profitable to make? Any manufacturer of a product would fall into this category. I would also include here a product as being a physical location (the product you are analyzing is the store economics itself). For example, a Lululemon retail store would be an example, as would a Whole Foods.

The Layers of the Unit

There are many layers you can drill into within a unit, and this is where the gold of strategic insight will reveal itself. What about the unit economics of certain products or product lines within the Lululemon store? What about the unit economics of GoPro's retail vs. website channel for selling and distribution? For a service firm, what happens when you sell a web design product versus a consulting project? Unit economics can help you answer all of these questions and more.

As you get more familiar and comfortable with these concepts and gather the data you need, you'll be able to move down the learning curve of experience and control more quickly. Moving down the learning curve means increasing specificity in your unit analysis (e.g., from the company level to the line of business level to the specific client level).

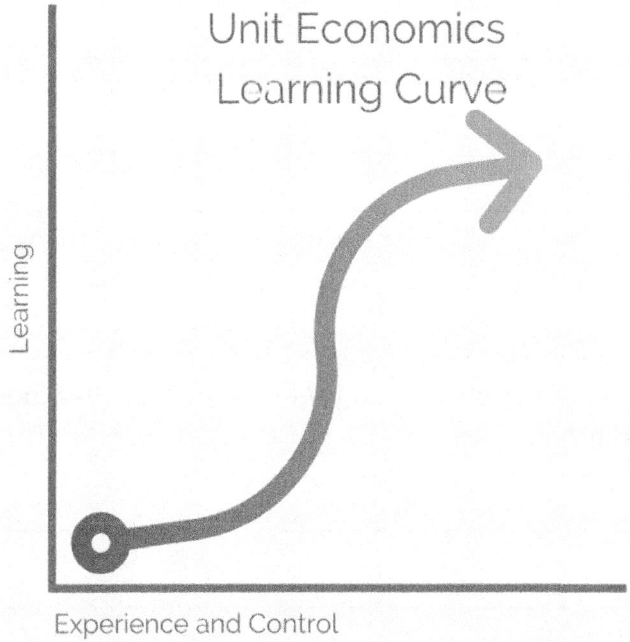

Many entrepreneurs are used to operating on instinct, great looks, and unbridled infectious enthusiasm. While that will get you somewhere for a while, it's not the same as building a sustainable business machine. Instinct might get your business off the ground, but it's the controls and levers of business fundamentals like unit economics that will keep you in the air.

Your Unit Model Exercise

Spend five to 10 minutes writing down answers to the following questions about your business:

1. What is the unit model of your business?

____

____

____

____

2. How deeply do you understand your unit model today?

____

____

____

____

3. What don't you know that you wish you did?

____

____

____

____

4. What could you do if you understood your unit model even more thoroughly?

____

____

____

____

Chapter Summary

In this chapter, we've covered the basics of unit economics, unit types, and the importance of getting a handle on your company's unit economics.

- Revenue - variable costs = unit economics.
- You cannot scale a business if you don't have profitable unit economics.
- A unit can be a customer (think Netflix), a service (think marketing agencies), or a product (think GoPro).
- Your unit economics can help you ask and answer high-level, strategic questions about your business.

In chapter two, we'll dig a little deeper into the anatomy of unit economics.

2. THE ANATOMY OF UNIT ECONOMICS

In this chapter, we're going to jump directly into the anatomy of unit economics. I will explore the underbelly of calculating unit economics and describe how to set up your financial statements to make them more actionable. When we talk about financial statements for unit economic analysis, we are referring to the income statement, the scorecard of your revenue and expenses in a given period.

Unfortunately, many businesses use financial statements only as a vehicle for looking backward, rather than a tool for looking forward and making decisions. The way your income statement and its underlying detail are structured can give you control and power, and act as a lever for helping you use your financials to make better strategic decisions.

Getting Answers from Your Financials

Back in 2005, I was raising money for my first company, REM Medical, which offered health care services and operated several clinics. While raising funds, I went to the office of Kurt Dammeier, who started some very notable companies in Seattle. During the meeting, Kurt sat back in his chair and threw me a marker as I stood at a white board. He said, "Walk me through your unit economics."

I panicked a bit. It was the perfect question, but I was perfectly unprepared. I fumbled a bit but survived. Kurt really wanted to understand a few things:

1. What are your fixed versus variable costs?
2. What is your contribution margin?
3. What is your break-even point?

Fixed Vs. Variable Costs

First, he wanted to understand my fixed costs and how those fixed costs would change as my business grew.

- **Fixed costs** are costs that do not vary with revenue growth, such as expenses related to rent, admin/management payroll, or facilities and equipment.

Second, he wanted to understand which costs would grow directly as I generated more revenue. Those costs are called variable costs.

- **Variable costs** are costs that vary with sales, like variable cost labor, sales commissions, or direct advertising.

Contribution Margin

Third, he wanted to know how profitable each location would be as well as the profitability of each patient that we served. In other words, he wanted to know my revenue less my variable costs. That figure is the contribution margin.

- **Contribution margin** is revenue less the variable costs to generate that revenue.

ALERT! ALERT! When we talk about unit economics, we are really talking about command over your contribution margin. While this is a new term, it is going to become an essential calculation. Don't forget CONTRIBUTION MARGIN!

Break-Even Point

Thc final insight that Kurt was looking for was an understanding of how long it would take before my contribution margin would cover my fixed costs. Before that, I'd be losing money. After that, I'd be generating a profit for the company. When my contribution margin equals my fixed costs, that's when I hit break-even.

- **Break-even** is the point at which your contribution margin is equal to your fixed costs. After you reach the break-even marker, you can begin to generate profits.

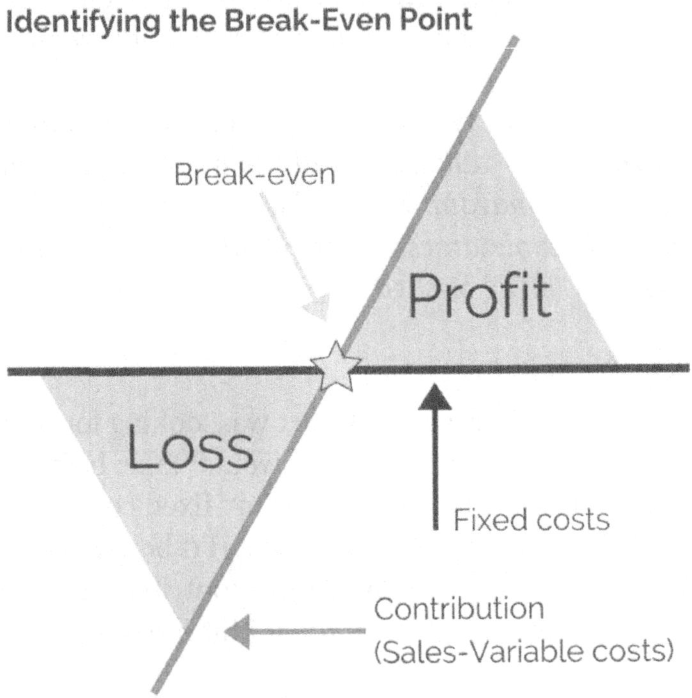

How Does This Information Aid Strategic Decision Making?

Although the concepts here are quite simple, it's often incredibly hard for businesses to answer questions like Kurt's because of the way financial statements are set up. The data can be very hard to tease out. However, you can find answers to these questions with a small amount of information—using the unit economics levers we'll discuss in this chapter.

Even with this very simple understanding, you can start to ask questions like:

- If I can reduce my variable costs, how will that reduce my time to break-even?
- If I can reduce my fixed costs, how much faster can I get to break-even?

Let's dig into this in more detail by looking at a case study.

Blast: A Case Study

While unit economics may make sense in the abstract, it will be easier to understand how it all works once we've put some real numbers behind it. I want to walk you through the financial statements of a hypothetical company called Blast. Blast is a marketing firm that primarily sells marketing consulting projects.

First, let's look at what you might consider to be a traditional income statement.

Basic Income Statement	2019
Revenue	$500,00
Cost of Goods Sold (COGS)	250,000
Gross Profit	**250,000**
Expenses	
Salaries and Benefits	125,000
Rent and Overhead	50,000
Depreciation and Amortization	3,500
Interest	8,000
Total Expenses	**186,500**
Earnings Before Tax	**63,500**
Taxes	10,000
Net Earnings	**$53,500**

Now, the problem with traditional income statements like this one is that they don't actually tell you all that much. For the most part you can look at margins (defined as expenses or profit line items divided by revenue) For example:

1. **Gross profit is 50%.** Gross profit is defined as revenue minus cost of goods sold divided by revenue. Gross profit is represented most often on a company-wide level where the cost of goods sold are the direct costs (not always variable) associated with generating that revenue.
    a. ($500,000-$250,000)/$500,000 (revenue minus the cost of goods sold, gross profit divided by revenue).

2. **Earnings Before Tax (EBT) margin is 12.7%.** EBT is "earnings before taxes," which is an easier way to assess the profitability of a business in comparison to others in your industry because tax structures can be different depending on the type of your corporate organization.
    a. The EBT is calculated in this instance as $63,500/$500,000.

But with a little manipulation (like reorganizing certain expense categories), we can unlock a bit more interesting data. Any bookkeeper or accountant should be able to create a statement like this for you.

Reorganized Income Statement	2019
Revenue	$500,000
Cost of Goods Sold (COGS)	250,000
Gross Profit	**250,000**
Expenses	
Salaries and Benefits	125,000
Rent and Overhead	50,000
EBITDA	75,000
Depreciation & Amortization	3,500
EBIT	71,500
Interest	8,000
Earnings Before Tax	63,500
Taxes	10,000
Net Earnings	**$53,500**

This statement can tell you some things, for example:

1. **EBITDA margin is 15%. EBITDA** is earnings before interest, tax, depreciation and amortization. EBITDA is used to analyze the performance of a company's core operations without the costs of the capital structure and tax expenses impacting profit or the accounting decisions (e.g., how are we choosing to depreciate?). EBITDA becomes especially relevant as a multiple when buying and selling businesses. You might hear the

phrase that companies are purchased for a multiple of EBITDA (e.g., 4x).

   a. EBITDA margin is calculated here as $75,000/$500,000.

2. **EBIT margin is 14.3%.** EBIT is earnings before interest and tax. EBIT is often used by creditors as a proxy for cash when they're trying to figure out how much debt your business can absorb, and what your ability is to repay interest. EBIT can also be used for comparing your company to others in your industry, by eliminating the interest and tax variable.
   a. The EBIT is calculated in this instance as $71,500/$500,000.

Are any of these results good or bad? Are they actionable? It's almost impossible to know from the statement alone. The statement might allow Blast's founder to ask some questions of their accountant, management, or CFO, like, "I wonder how we can improve gross margin or reduce overhead?" It might be helpful if Blast was benchmarking these metrics vs. other companies like theirs, but that's about it—there's just not a lot to go on here.

The standard income statement and the revised income statement above are not informative enough. These template income statements are common, but they do not offer the strategic insights based on unit economics that allow for fact-based decision-making.

Calculating Contribution Margin

Early warning, this final and more detailed version income statement has a lot more numbers—let's glance at it, and then walk through this one step at a time. I don't want you to look at this statement and think you need to figure out how to create this. What you need to do is ask the right questions of the experts around you to get this information.

Detailed and Actionable Income Statement	2019
Revenue	**$500,000**
Cost of Goods Sold (COGS)	
Software	60,000
Contract Labor – Customer Service	65,000
Consultant Payroll	125,000
Total Cost of Goods Sold	250,000
Gross Profit	**250,000**
Expenses	
Payroll	
Wages – Admin	54,000
Wages – Sales	30,000
Wages – Marketing	25,000
Bonuses and Commissions	5,000
Benefits – Admin	5,000
Benefits – Sales	3,000
Benefits – Marketing	3,000
Total Payroll	125,000
Marketing	
Advertising	2,500
Overhead (G&A)	47,500
Depreciation and Amort.	3,500

Interest	8,000
Earnings Before Tax	**63,500**
Taxes	10,000
Net Earnings	**$53,500**

One of the benefits of this more detailed income statement is that Blast can now easily calculate the contribution margin. The formula for calculating contribution margin is revenue minus variable costs. Let's see what that looks like for Blast.

Finding Contribution Margin

Blast's revenue is $500,000 and the variable costs are $257,500.

- Variable costs include payroll associated with generating that revenue, software costs that grow as revenue increases, variable sales commissions and direct advertising.
    - $500,000 - $257,500 = $242,500.
- Contribution for Blast is $242,500.
- This means Blast generates $242,500 of unit profit for its marketing engagements.

A quick note about payroll, here. Blast pays its employees a full-time salary, so you might think it should not be considered a variable cost. However, because Blast is a service business whose revenue is driven by hours worked, the salary for those employees responsible for producing the revenue should be considered a variable cost. Bonuses and commissions will vary with sales, and advertising is tied to driving conversion and sales. In general, if there is some fuzziness around classification, err on the side of calling it a variable cost. That is a more conservative approach.

Finding Contribution Margin Percentage

Blast's contribution margin is $242,500. To calculate the contribution margin percentage, divide the contribution by Blast's revenue.

- $242,500÷500,000 = 48.5%.

This means that for every $1 of revenue that Blast generates, the company spends $0.515 in variable costs, leaving $0.485 profit to cover fixed costs.

Fixed Costs and Payroll

Blast's fixed costs will include rent and some payroll costs, as well as marketing and facility costs not specifically associated with generating revenue. When thinking about fixed costs, remember that it doesn't matter whether or not revenue is generated, because those costs will not vary. From a practical standpoint, of course, fixed costs will rise over time as revenue increases, but it is more of a step than a linear function.

Operating Leverage

We can see from the contribution margin calculation of 48.5% that Blast has low operating leverage. Operating leverage is the degree to which a company can increase operating profit while increasing income. For Blast, it says that for every dollar of revenue it generates above break-even, it contributes $.485 to operating profit. In some software companies, you might see a contribution margin that's closer to 80%, rather than 48.5%. Why? Well, selling software alone does not require a lot of additional labor. It can be very profitable, but there are trade-offs.

In a lower operating leverage environment such as Blast, the business is a bit less risky. It's easier to reach the break-even point, because you have fewer fixed costs sitting underneath those variable costs. It's less likely that you'll go out of business because you burned a lot of cash just to keep the doors open.

On the flip side, once you hit the break-even point, you're not going to generate as much profit. High operating leverage environments like software companies get valued so highly because, for those companies that become home-run tech businesses, there is immense profit to be had once the fixed costs are covered. Blast is a service business, meaning the company is not as likely to see immense, quick profits—but they also reduce some of their downside risk.

A Quick Reflection

I want to pause on this case study to really emphasize the benefits when we get just that little bit of additional detail. In the detailed income statement, we were able to see the business as a whole. With that level of information, we can ask much more detailed questions and make much more strategic choices.

The best part is that this is something that your bookkeeper or accounting partner can set up for you. You should be able to have your revenue and costs classified so that you can see everything that's happening at the project level. Blast will be able to ask questions like, "What is the unit profitability for the web design projects versus the consulting projects?" or, "What is the unit profitability when we just sell our analytics software as a standalone?" This is what I mean by moving down the learning curve.

The more we break apart the financials and dig into the individual product and service lines, the more value we can extract, but we have to start by gaining command over the contribution margin, which you have done. Armed with just a little bit of information, we can start asking and answering questions like, "What's the break-even point for this business?" Let's go there next.

Calculating Blast's Break-even

In Blast's case, they sell marketing projects. I created the table below to build up revenue by number of projects sold and average revenue per project. Notice that, on average, Blast generates $10,000 per project and sold 50 projects last year. With information we already have, we will be able to quickly see how many deals Blast would need to close to break even in their business.

Calculating Variable Cost Per Unit

Let's turn to the variable cost per project. We know Blast's variable costs are $257,000. We also know they've sold 50 projects. That means Blast's variable cost per project is $5,150 ($257,500/50).

Break-Even Units and Revenue	2019
Revenue	
# of Projects Sold This Year	50
Average Revenue per Project	$10,000
Total Revenue	$500,000
Variable Costs	257,500
Contribution Margin	**242,500**
Contribution Margin %	48.5%
Fixed Operating Expenses	179,000
Fixed OpEx Margin %	35.8%
Earnings Before Tax	$63,500
Earnings Before Tax Margin %	12.7%

Calculating Contribution Margin Per Unit

To generate $10,000 of revenue, Blast incurs variable costs of $5,150. The contribution margin per unit here is pretty easy to figure out: subtract variable costs from revenue.

- $10,000 - $5,150 = $4,850.

Calculating Break-Even

Blast also has $179,000 of fixed operating expenses or fixed costs. To cover that $179,000 of fixed costs (to reach break-even), how many projects need to be sold? The break-even point, then, is Blast's fixed operating expenses divided by the contribution margin per unit.

- $179,000÷ $4,850 = 37.

When Blast has generated 37 projects, they break even. How much revenue is that?

On average, remember, Blast sells for $10,000 each.

- $10,000 × 37 = $370,000.

At $370,000 of revenue, Blast had a break-even business. We can prove this:

37 projects x $10,000 (Revenue per Project)	$370,000
37 projects x $4,850 (Contribution Margin)	$179,000
Fixed costs	($179,000)
Operating Profit	$0

Note: small adjustments for rounding

Analyzing Profit Impact at Different Project Volumes

A table like the one below can be constructed to show how much more operating income could be generated at higher units, or how much is lost at fewer units sold. This type of information can be strategically valuable.

How can Blast reduce its variable costs and drive a higher profit per project or unit sold? How could your company do the same?

# Sold	Sales	Var. Costs	Cont. Margin	Fixed Costs	Op. Income
10	$100,000	$51,500	$48,500	$179,000	($130,500)
20	200,000	103,000	97,000	179,000	(82,000)
30	300,000	154,500	145,500	179,000	(33,500)
37	370,000	191,000	179,000	179,000	-
50	500,000	257,500	242,500	179,000	63,500
75	750,000	386,250	363,750	179,000	184,750
100	1M	515,000	485,000	179,000	306,000

Note: small adjustments for rounding

Variable Cost Exercise

Think about your own business and the levers you have available to reduce your break-even point. Remember, the faster you get to break-even, the faster you start to generate profit. Even if you are past break-even today, how could you reduce your variable costs so that you generate more profit per engagement? Below, list three opportunities to reduce your variable costs.

1.

____

____

2.

____

____

3.

____

____

Chapter Summary

We covered a lot of ground in this chapter, including fixed and variable expenses, contribution margin, break-even point, the importance of a detailed income statement, some of the key questions to ask of your financials, and how to start calculating answers to those questions.

- Fixed costs are costs that do not vary with revenue growth, including expenses like rent, admin/management payroll, or facilities and equipment.
- Variable costs are costs that vary with sales, like variable cost labor, or sales commissions, or direct advertising.
- Contribution margin is revenue less the variable costs to generate that revenue. You find your contribution margin by dividing contribution costs by revenue:
    - Contribution ÷ Revenue = Contribution margin.
- Break-even is the point at which your contribution margin is equal to your fixed costs. After you reach break-even, you generate profits. You can find your break-even point by dividing your operating expenses by your contribution margin per unit:
    - Operating expenses ÷Contribution margin per unit = Units needed to reach break-even.

The biggest elephant in the room for most professional service businesses is how to measure the effectiveness of labor. We will discuss this critical area of unit economics in the next chapter.

3. LABOR EFFICIENCY

For most of you, labor is your number one cost of sale, the most expensive resource in your business. Managing labor is the holy grail of your business but is often the one that is the least understood. It is hard to measure the effectiveness of individual labor units and many shy away from it. Understanding your labor inputs through labor efficiency ratios will not only give you more unit economic insight, but will also create a more transparent work environment.

There are two types of labor efficiency ratios: direct labor and management labor. I want to take a moment to calculate these labor efficiency ratios so you can see how they work in practice. Again, this is something for you to ask of your bookkeeper and accountant. You can tell them, "I want to look at my income statement in such a way that I can calculate labor efficiency." Breaking out profit and loss statements in this way allows you to be more informed—all you have to do is classify your costs in a way that allows you to extract this information. Again, your bookkeeper or account should be able to do this for you.

Direct Labor Efficiency Ratio

The formula for **direct labor efficiency ratio** (DLER) involves what we call non-labor gross margin, which is revenue minus non-labor cost of goods sold. In a service business, you're probably not going to have a lot of non-labor costs. In Blast's case, they have some software costs. To calculate DLER, divide your non-labor gross margin by direct labor costs. Let's look at an example of what that might look like in practice based on Blast's numbers from the case study.

P&L for the Direct Labor Efficiency Ratio	2019
Revenue	$500,000
Cost of Goods Sold (non-labor)	60,000
Gross Margin (non-labor)	440,000
Gross Margin %	88%
Direct Labor	190,000
Other Variable Costs	7,500
Contribution Margin	242,500
Contribution Margin %	49%
Admin/Management Labor	120,000
Other Expenses	59,000
Operating Income	$63,500

Calculating Direct Labor Efficiency Ratio

To determine the direct labor efficiency ratio, divide $440,000 by $190,000.

- 440,000 ÷190,000 = 2.3.

What does that mean? It means that for every $1 of direct labor, Blast generates $2.30 of gross margin.

Management Labor Efficiency Ratio

The **management labor efficiency ratio** (MLER) is the contribution margin divided by the administrative or management labor.

To calculate MLER, divide your contribution margin by admin/management labor costs labor costs.

Management labor is typically the salaries of the CEO, sales and marketing, product or R&D, HR, etc. These are positions that aren't directly tied to the generation of the revenue. Don't get me wrong, you're important and all, you're just classified differently for the purposes of this calculation.

Let's look at the same P&L again as shared above from Blast, with management labor numbers this time.

P&L for the Management Labor Efficiency Ratio	2019
Revenue	$500,000
Cost of Goods Sold (non-labor)	60,000
Gross Margin (non-labor)	440,000
Gross Margin %	88%
Direct Labor	190,000
Other Variable Costs	7,500
Contribution Margin	242,500
Contribution Margin %	49%
Admin/Management Labor	120,000
Other Expenses	59,000
Operating Income	$63,500

Calculating Management Labor Efficiency Ratio

In this case, Blast's management labor efficiency ratio is $242,500 divided by $120,000.

- $242,500 ÷120,000 = 2.1.

For every $1 of administrative or management labor, Blasts generates $2.10 of contribution margin.

In isolation, these labor efficiency numbers are meaningless. Typically, labor efficiency ratios are measured over time to look at trends. The specificity of these ratios, as you will see later, can drill into specific individuals and their efficiency on various projects. Once you get a good handle on your labor efficiency, you are going to make some incredibly smart business decisions. Tracked over time, these numbers start to paint a picture that will give you confidence in your labor utilization decision-making.

Using Labor Efficiency to Evaluate the Cost of Hiring a Salesperson

Let’s think about how we might use labor efficiency data to evaluate the impact of hiring a salesperson. I want to work through this relatively slowly and somewhat methodically because I don't want you to be overwhelmed by the numbers or by the data. I don't need you, as I said, to become the expert in exactly how these are sourced. I need you to know why these matter, and they matter.

Stay with me. Blast is going to add a $200,000 salesperson. What does that new hire need to produce in order for Blast to maintain, all things being equal, the same labor efficiency ratios? Let’s take a look at Blast’s potential P&L statement with the new hire, one step at a time.

Step 1: Set Up Your Table and Input What You Know Right Now

You know that you are going to add a salesperson. You also know that you intend to maintain the same gross margin % and contribution margin %. The question marks are what we want to answer.

Also, remember that we want to maintain the same level of labor efficiency. Recall that we calculated labor efficiencies as follows:

- Direct Labor Efficiency Ratio (DLER): 2.3.
- Management Labor Efficiency Ratio (MLER): 2.1.

P&L for the Labor Efficiency Ratio: New Hire Scenario			**2019**
Category	Original Amount	With new Hire	End Result
Revenue COGS (non-labor)	$500,00 60,000		??
Gross Margin (non-labor) *Gross Margin %*	440,000 *88%*		**??** *88%*
Direct Labor	190,000		**??**
Other Variable Costs	7,500		**??**
Contribution Margin *Contribution Margin %*	242,500 *49%*		**??** *49%*
Admin/Management Labor	120,000	200,000	320,000
Other Expenses	59,000	0	59,000
Operating Income	$63,000		**$??**

Step 2. Calculate Contribution Margin

Blast wants to calculate the contribution margin. In order to do this, we will take the management labor of $320,000 and multiply it by the management labor efficiency ratio (2.1). This produces a contribution margin of $666,667. So, when adding that $200,000 salesperson, we will be looking to achieve a contribution margin of $666,667.

Contribution Margin			**2019**
Category	Original Amount	With New Hire	End Result
Contribution Margin *Contribution Margin %*	$242,500 *49%*		**$666,667** *49%*

Step 3: Calculate Revenue

We know Blast has a contribution margin percentage of 48.5%. We also know the updated contribution margin: $666,667. To calculate required revenue, we will divide $666,667 by 48.5% to get $1,374,500. Or said another way, revenue of $1,374,500 multiplied by 48.5% = $666,667.

Adding this salesperson means Blast needs to increase revenue by $874,500.

Revenue			**2019**
Category	Original Amount	With new Hire	End Result
Revenue	$500,000	**+$874,000**	$1,374,500

Step 4: Calculate Non-Labor Gross Margin

To maintain that same non-labor gross margin percentage of 88%, Blast is going to have a gross margin of $1.209 million.

Non-Labor Gross Margin Sales			**2019**
Category	Original Amount	With new Hire	End Result
Gross Margin (non-labor) *Gross Margin %*	$440,000 *88%*		**$1,209,622** *88%*

Step 5: Calculate Direct Labor Costs

Now let's calculate Blast's direct labor costs. When we hire a salesperson and we say to that salesperson, "Person, you're going to have to generate some serious revenue," we as the business owner have a responsibility to support the growth in sales with direct labor. Blast is going to have to hire some people.

So, remember, Blast has a direct labor efficiency ratio of 2.3, which says that for every $1 of direct labor, they generate $2.30 cents of non-labor gross margin. We know that the non-labor gross margin is $1.209 million. So, Blast's direct labor is going to be:

- $1.209 million ÷2.3 = $522,337.

Let's check our calculation in another way: if we took Blast's non-labor gross margin of $1.2 million and divided it by $522,000, it equals 2.3.

Direct Labor			**2019**
Category	Original Amount	With new Hire	End Result
Direct Labor	$190,000	**+$332,000**	$522,337

Step 6: Put it all Together

What all of this means is that for Blast to add a salesperson for $200,000 and maintain the same labor efficiency standards, the new salesperson needs to drive $874,000 in revenue. Blast also needs to be prepared to incur an additional $332,000 in direct labor costs to support that expected growth in sales. Is that good? Is it realistic? I have no idea. It's interesting, though, right? Blast is a service business. For a service business to go hire what looks like a pretty expensive person on a fixed salary when they only have a contribution margin of 48.5% is a tall order. That hire has got to generate a lot of revenue to cover themselves.

Adjusted P&L for the Labor Efficiency Ratio: New Hire Scenario			**2019**
Category	Original Amount	With new Hire	End Result
Revenue COGS (non-labor)	$500,00 60,000	+ **$874,000 Sales**	$1,374,500 164,948
Gross Margin (non-labor) *Gross Margin %*	440,000 *88%*		**1,209,622** *88%*
Direct Labor	190,000	+~ **$332,000 Labor**	**522,337**
Other Variable Costs	7,500		13,622
Contribution Margin *Contribution Margin %*	242,500 *49%*		**666,667** *49%*
Admin/ Management Labor	120,000	+ **$200,000 Sales person**	320,000
Other Expenses	59,000		59,000
Operating Income	$63,500		$287,667

Here's the thing: Regardless of what decision you make when doing your calculations, you now have the data to have the strategic conversation. You have the data to ask, "What does this person need to accomplish? What do we need to be prepared for if we're going to hire this person?" Again, the goal here isn't for you to become the master in the calculation detail.

But I do want to impress upon you that when you make an investment decision, the implications of that investment can be filtered through your financial statements so that you can be better grounded in making a strategic business decision based on fact, and not on emotion.

As business leaders we are, by design, emotionally driven and emotionally charged individuals. When we take the emotion, the chutzpah, and the energy that got us to where we are now and complement them with a data-driven and data-rich approach to decision making, we become unstoppable. We garner more confidence in our decisions, especially during times of uncertainty.

Chapter Summary

Right now, you might be asking, "What just happened to me?" What just happened to you is that you nailed the contribution margin. Congratulations! You grasped labor efficiency. Woot! You ran a couple of scenarios that will enable you to use your financials to ask questions in a way that you may know instinctively, but maybe have never seen laid out like this before.

- The direct labor efficiency ratio involves non-labor gross margin, which is revenue minus non-labor cost of goods sold. In a service business, you're probably not going to have a lot of non-labor costs.
    - Non-labor gross margin ÷ Direct labor costs = Direct labor efficiency ratio.
- The management labor efficiency ratio is the contribution margin divided by your administrative labor costs.
    - Contribution margin ÷ Administrative labor costs = Management labor efficiency ratio.
- You can use labor efficiency ratios to calculate the cost of strategic business decisions, hiring choices, and more.

Some things to consider: Pay close attention to your chart of accounts. How your accounting line items are structured matters a lot. All of these details matter, and time tracking, which we'll discuss in the next chapter, allows you to get even more specific.

When you can start allocating different people to different projects and lines of business and geography, then you start peeling the layers of the onion back to get the specificity that you need. And remember: if you're going to measure labor efficiency ratios, measure them over time.

4. TIME TRACKING: THE HOLY GRAIL OF UNIT ECONOMICS

In this chapter, I want to talk about the holy grail of unit economics: time tracking. When labor is your most expensive cost of sale and you don't have a grasp of how well you are utilizing that cost, it's time to make a shift. And the shift is getting a deeper understanding of how your labor is being utilized—and that is best measured through time tracking.

Behavioral Science Shows Why Labor Costs Are Tough to Manage

There are two behavioral science laws that make it risky to manage people in a service organization without tracking time well.

Parkinson's Law

Parkinson's Law says that work expands to fill the time available. Give someone a task and an hour, and it'll take an hour for the work to get done. Give someone the same task and 15 minutes, and they'll do that same task in 15 minutes. In other words, there is no way to improve efficiency if we aren't tracking time and if we aren't putting constraints on how much time is available to complete a task.

Parkinson's Law says that, by nature, work is going to fill the time available. We probably know that holds true in our personal lives, and we can see how that plays out in our professional lives, too.

Hofstadter's Law

Hofstadter's Law states that things always take longer than expected, even when we know they will take longer than expected. That remains true even when you know Hofstadter's Law and you say, "I know Hofstadter's Law. It's going to take longer than expected. Let's put a buffer in because it's going to take longer than expected." It will still take longer than expected.

Humans are, to be blunt, super bad at estimating how long something is going to take. We just don't know how long something will take unless we measure how long it actually takes.

The fear we have around measurement of people's time hamstrings our ability to build a machine that's going to transcend us as business leaders. When we don't have a good handle on our cost of sales, it's hard for us as business owners to really have confidence that we can work on our business. So instead, we work in it. The gateway to better decision-making is to track time. It just is.

Excuses for Not Tracking Time

Of course, there are a lot of reasons why people think they can't track time in their business, but for many, not doing it is really just the path of least resistance. I have conversations with prospects and clients all the time. They'll say things like, "We don't have a culture of time tracking," or, "We tried it before, and it didn't work out." If someone is building a lifestyle business and wants to make just enough to support their family, that's fine. It can be an awesome way to build a lifestyle business.

However, if you're building a machine that can transcend you and build real equity value, time tracking becomes essential. Ask yourself, "Okay, which lens am I going to wear? What is the type of organization that I want to build?" That's going to drive some of your decision-making here.

We often hear that it's hard to ask people to track time when you want them spending their time being creative. That's probably the number one comment that Stride hears from our agency clients, and we understand that it feels that way to many people. For us, we want to share how time tracking is a benefit for our clients, and by extension, their employees. How does time tracking create an environment that creates more space for you?

What we have actually found is that time tracking creates:

- *more* time,
- *more* support,
- *cleaner* handoffs,
- *less* ambiguity,
- *less* distraction,
- *reduced* variability.

What Time Tracking Does For The Business Owner

Here's what time tracking enables: Time tracking enables more control over client and project level profitability. It allows you to better engage your clients in fact-based discussions—you have the data. It empowers your team to build their plan based on the time available for the budgeted engagement. Time tracking helps to better plan for staffing. For those of you that are developing software products, isolating out your R&D helps when you're calculating tax credits. There's real money involved, along with transparency in workloads, handoffs, and timelines.

Let's take a look at a real example. This is a visualization for one of our clients at Stride. Stride provides virtual back-office, bookkeeping, and accounting services for hundreds of clients around the country on a fixed fee basis. While we do not charge by the hour, it is essential that we understand how we are using time based on our projected estimates.

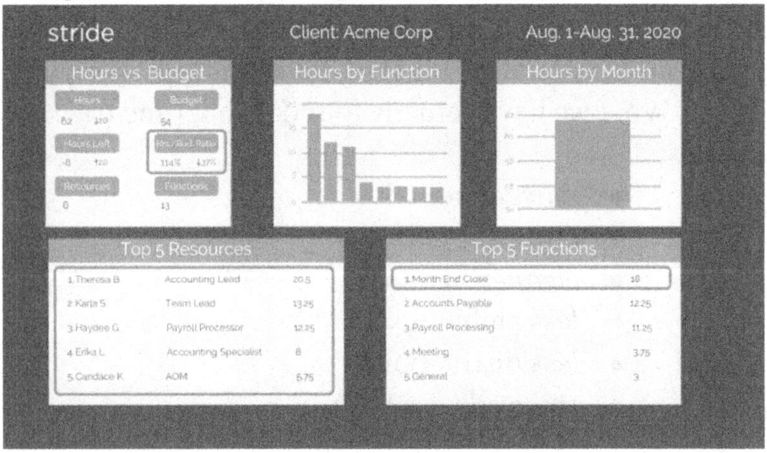

To create this dashboard, we pulled time tracking into a data warehouse where we can start asking questions. This product, called Stride Vista, creates transparency of information that helps us make smarter business decisions for client management.

What you can see in this visual are several pieces of information:

1. We're over budget on time in August.
2. Month-end close work is taking the longest amount of time.
3. We have five resources for this project and the staffing mix is high.

Can you see the room for a data-driven conversation here? We might even be able to say to the client, "Hey, we want to work with you on a win-for-all. This is not a win-for-all right now. Let's figure out how and why. It may be because the scope of the engagement with you is increased, and we haven't changed the price. It could be because there's room for efficiency."

What we have found is that approaching clients with a data-driven approach to the conversation, stories get grounded with facts. You let go of the emotion and you drive towards a rational outcome that benefits your business and clients.

Uses for Time Tracking

Where unit economics gets really interesting is when you can start looking at your units of production and making informed decisions. As mentioned before, you can break labor efficiency down by team, by customer, or by project type.

Labor Efficiency by Team

Direct Labor Efficiency Ratio by Team Member	
Mary	2.25
John	2.50
Rick	1.75
Sam	3.00

Tracking information like this allows you to ask questions like, "Is Rick flailing, based on these numbers? For every dollar of labor that Rick incurs, we're only generating $1.75 in non-labor gross margin compared to Sam at $3.00," or, "Is Sam killing it, or is he completely overworked and about to quit?" "What about the projects Rick and Sam run? What's going on there?"

Labor Efficiency by Customer

Direct Labor Efficiency Ratio by Customer	
Wilson Sports	3.20
Shopify	2.85
Shake Shack	2.25
Bob's Hardware	1.55

If you look at these figures by customer, you can look at the people that are associated with serving customers. "Is Bob's an unprofitable client? The labor efficiency ratio is really low. Have we raised prices recently?" or "Is this even a good industry for us to be working in? Are we pricing correctly for these types of clients in this industry?"

Labor Efficiency by Project

Direct Labor Efficiency Ratio by Project Type	
Social Media	1.80
Consulting	1.50
Web Dev	2.80

You can even look at this information on specific projects. You might ask, "Should we shutter that consulting business?" Well, maybe not, because if consulting is the loss leader that gets you the web development projects, then you're not going to go close the consulting business. At least you're asking the question and can start digging into the data to find answers.

Implementing Time Tracking

There are a number of steps to take to make time tracking worthwhile.

First, implement a time tracking system. We have had success with Harvest and TSheets but there are many on the market.

Second, build the WIIFY (What's In It For You) for your team, so that they understand the benefits of time tracking. This might include a better workload, increased support, etc. You can't provide the WIIFY without the data that time tracking will offer. Position the time tracking in a way that helps their workload and see how transparency actually improves the quality of results. Work with your bookkeeper or accountant to put together an analysis that tracks the time at a project level.

Third, commit to the ratios. Go back to the direct and management labor efficiency ratios from the previous chapter and think about how having a better understanding of time at the employee, customer, and project level will enable you to make strategic business decisions.

Chapter Summary

In this chapter, we've covered the reasons that time tracking matters, common excuses for not tracking time, the actual benefits time tracking provides, and offered some tools to get you started.

- Parkinson's Law says work expands to fill the time available.
- Hofstadter's Law says things always take longer than expected, even when we know they will take longer than expected. (That remains true even when you know Hofstadter's Law.)
- Excuses for not tracking time often include cultural concerns and prior failures.
- The benefits of time tracking outweigh those excuses, and include better control of time and data, support, clarity, less distraction, and the ability to engage in data-driven conversations with clients.
- Time tracking allows you to understand labor efficiency by team, customer, and project.
- There are many tools available for time tracking.

In the next bonus chapter, we will look at unit economics for recurring revenue business models. Many businesses today would like to have more predictable, recurring revenue. We'll talk about how to manage and measure that.

5. BONUS CHAPTER: UNIT ECONOMICS FOR RECURRING REVENUE BUSINESSES

Your business may generate revenue on a recurring revenue basis. In that case, you are acquiring the customer (as the unit) and the customer is paying you predictably over time. You paid to acquire them and now you've got to keep them, because that's where you generate profit, but maybe only months from now. I want to talk about that kind of business, because it's a really attractive business model.

Recurring Revenue

Recurring revenue is any product or service that customers purchase on a predictable basis. You know that once you acquire the customer, month in and month out, the revenue will recur. This is different from, say, a grocery store. Someone might go to the grocery store once a week, but it's not recurring revenue, because it's somewhat unpredictable. Someone might have regular purchases, but irregular patterns. That model is not recurring.

What makes recurring revenue so attractive is that it allows for more consistency. You can do some cool things, including planning your business with more predictability. You won't go into every month saying, "How am I going to generate revenue this month?" and there are many businesses that start each month not knowing where that revenue will come from. Recurring revenue eliminates that uncertainty.

A recurring revenue model allows you to better manage your metrics. You can build relationships with customers, because you actually sell to the customer twice: you sell to acquire them initially, and then you keep selling to maintain the relationship and extend the lifetime value. A recurring revenue model means you might be a little bit less stressed as a business owner. You tend to be able to scale your business faster in that type of environment.

However, there are real risks to the recurring revenue model, too. The first risk as I mentioned is that you do have two sales to worry about: customer acquisition and customer retention. These sales tend to be expensive to scale, because you have to build a business machine just to keep that customer for a period of time: support and service, new features, keeping things fresh. A significant focus gets placed on retention, and there are a lot of metrics to manage in a recurring revenue business model. Let's take a look at an example.

Customer Acquisition

Here's a representation of the cash flow profile that a recurring revenue business might have of a single customer.

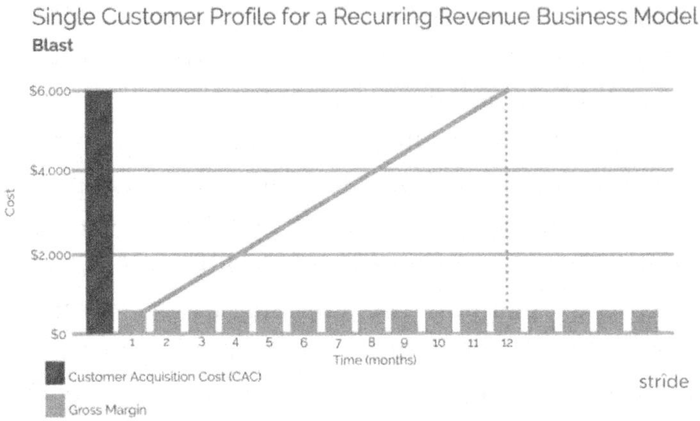

Let's say the customer acquisition cost (CAC) was $6,000. Every month after acquisition, I generate $500 of gross margin (remember: revenue - direct costs = gross margin). Since it cost me $6,000 to acquire this customer and the customer generates $500 per month, it will take 12 months for me to hit a break-even point with this customer.

Remember, this is just the one customer, every month. Now, let's think about the cash flow. For the first 12 months of the relationship with this client, I'm underwater. If I only have one customer in my business, I spent $6,000 to acquire them, and every month my cash flow will improve by $500. After 12 months, I'm going to break even.

Keep in mind that for this model, you have to fund the negative cash flow. You have to fund the $6,000 or whatever the CAC is, because you take a big hit up front and then get paid out a little bit every month. You're probably quite aware that really fast-growing, recurring revenue businesses require a lot of capital—this is why.

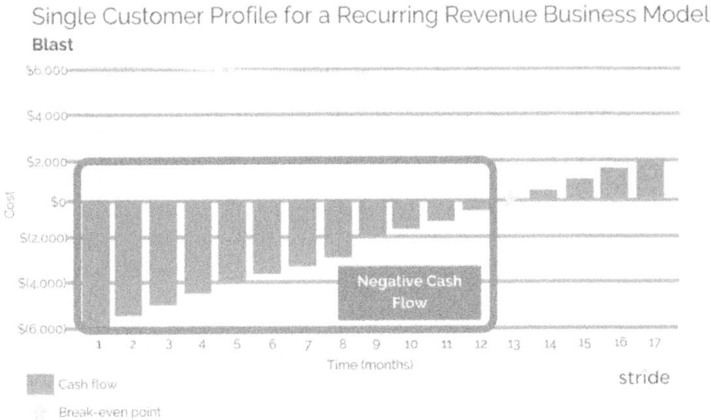

The more customers you bring on, the more capital it takes to acquire them. This is why many recurring revenue software businesses need a lot of capital to finance growth, because you have to fund customer acquisition. Even if your unit economics work out, you have to fund the upfront costs.

When considering your recurring revenue business, there are two magical rules that investors like to see. The first is that the cost to acquire a customer should be less than three times the value of that customer over their life. The second is that it should take less than 12 months to recover the cost of customer acquisition. For example, if I had a customer acquisition cost of $1,000, the lifetime value of that customer should be greater than $3,000. If my CAC was $1,200, the monthly recurring gross margin should be at least $100/month.

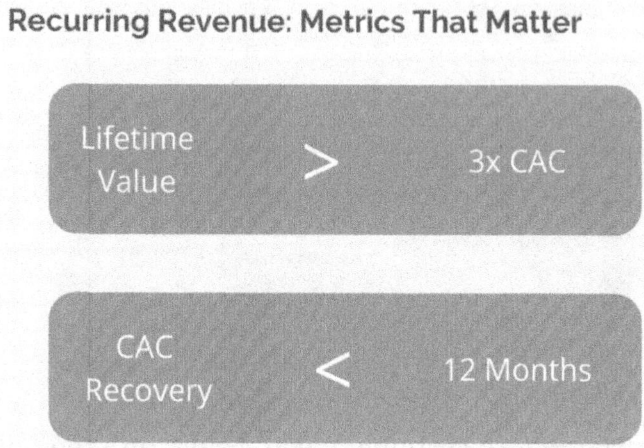

Calculating Customer Acquisition Cost

You also need to know how to calculate customer acquisition cost, and again, this is something you can pull out of your financials. In the simplest terms, **customer acquisition cost** is the sum of the total expenses deployed to acquire a customer (sales and marketing expenses, including labor), divided by the number of customers added in a given period, usually monthly. All of this data should be available in whatever financial tracking system you're using such as QuickBooks if it's set up correctly.

Let's look at an example of how to calculate this cost. Let's say sales and marketing costs in December amounted to $5,000, and in that month, the business added 50 customers. The customer acquisition cost works out to $100, which means the lifetime value for each customer needs to be greater than $300.

Sales & Marketing Costs	Customers Added	Customer Acquisition Cost	Lifetime Value Target
$5,000	50	$100	>$300

Calculating Lifetime Value

Lifetime value is the average recurring gross margin the business receives per month multiplied by how long the customer stayed with you. Sometimes people will use "average recurring revenue" vs. "average recurring gross margin" but remember that there are some direct costs associated with that revenue that should be considered. If a customer pays $50 per month, generates a gross margin of 90%, and stays with the business for 20 months, the lifetime value of that customer is $900.

- $50 x 90% gross margin = $45 monthly recurring revenue (MRR)
- $45 x 20 months = $900 lifetime value (LTV)

Quick Test: If I'm acquiring customers and the lifetime value of the customers is $900, I need to be looking pretty diligently at my customer acquisition costs and making sure I'm planning for the acquisition costs to be less than $300.

Payback Period

Payback period is the number of months it takes to recover your customer acquisition costs. The target payback period is 12 months. Let's use another example, assuming a monthly recurring revenue of $100 and a gross margin of 50%. In this case, the customer gross margin is $50. If the customer acquisition cost is $500, then the payback period is $500 ÷ $50, or 10 months.

MRR	Gross Margin %	Gross Margin Monthly	CAC	Payback Period
$100	50%	$50	500	10 Months

In this section, we've talked about customer acquisition costs for recurring revenue businesses. We've talked about lifetime value. We've talked about the payback period, and we looked at the profile of a single customer in the context of the unit economics—the economics of acquiring and keeping that customer. Now let's talk about churn.

Churn and Customer Retention

One last important topic is customer retention. Churn is the biggest evil or biggest bonanza in recurring revenue businesses. **Churn** is the amount of revenue, or the number of customers, lost in a given period. High churn is deadly. High churn is also a very sensitive metric. Companies that control their churn rate can experience amazing unit economics. Those that have high churn operate a leaky bucket that will eventually run out of water. Churn rate directly impacts the lifetime that a customer will stay with you.

Calculating Lifetime of a Customer in Months

There is a shortcut to calculate lifetime value by a group of customers:

1 / churn rate

Average Churn Rate	Customer Lifetime (Months)
1.5% per month	67 months
5% per month	20 months

Now, reflect for a minute on how much you invested to acquire that customer. Imagine if they leave before you hit break-even. Churn is so powerful and companies that figure out how to minimize it can experience enormous growth and profitability.

If you have a recurring revenue model, you want to design your business strategy around this question: How do I retain my customers? Retention is, of course, about delivering on your service promise, first and foremost. However, it's also about delivering that value (and more), consistently. Retaining customers, thus reducing churn, is what is going to drive a sustainable, profitable business for you.

Retention Exercise

Think about ways that you could retain your customers. List three strategies you could employ to reduce churn in your business.

1.

2.

3.

Chapter Summary

In this chapter, we covered some of the essential factors for recurring revenue businesses to consider, including the importance of customer acquisition, the payback period, churn, and customer retention.

- Recurring revenue is any product or service that customers purchase on a predictable basis.
- Customer acquisition can be especially expensive for businesses with recurring revenue, and it's important to know how to calculate the cost. The sum of the total expenses deployed to acquire a customer (sales and marketing expenses, including labor), divided by the number of customers added in a given period, usually monthly, will give you your customer acquisition cost.
    - Customer acquisition expenses ÷ Number of customers added = Customer acquisition cost.
- Payback period is the number of months it takes to recover your customer acquisition costs. The target payback period is 12 months.
- Churn is the amount of revenue, or the number of customers, lost in a given period.
    - 1 ÷ Churn Rate = Customer lifetime in months.
- Customer retention is of the utmost importance for recurring revenue.

CONCLUSIONS

Freedom as a business owner is about having trust and confidence that the machine you are building is running well, especially when you are not a required part of the machine. But so many entrepreneurs fear getting out of the machine because they don't know how it will run in their absence. They don't know what they can't measure and measurement in a business around financial performance demands a dive into unit economics. You have grasped the heartbeat of the machine in this book and now is your time to make it stronger than ever.

My hope is that you are more equipped to ask questions of your accounting or bookkeeping team because you now understand some core concepts like contribution margin and labor efficiency. My hope is that you double down on appreciating the benefits of time tracking. More than anything else, I want you energized to make some shifts in how you use your financial information as a strategic ally.

The key is to start out by identifying your fixed and variable costs. As you get more experienced, you want to be able to isolate your revenue and variable costs (i.e., contribution margin) at as simple of a unit as possible (e.g., a customer, a location, a business line). That's where you get power.

But remember that this is a journey. I do not need anybody to finish reading this book and immediately go into the micro-details of project-level profitability. Start off with a question like, “Can we get our fixed versus variable costs? Let's calculate our contribution margin at a business level first.”

Like anything else, hope is not a plan. You build a plan. You identify the factors that are going to make your plan come to fruition. And then you execute and learn. I am hopeful that this book spurs you to action.

We live in a world of running experiments and I would challenge you to have project-level profitability as one of the experiments that you want to run, because you believe that it is going to give you leverage in your business that you may not have had access to before or you believe can be enhanced.

We covered a lot of ground here and I'm proud that you arrived! Here's what we covered:

- We learned that unit economics is about freedom as an entrepreneur.
- We defined unit economics..
- We dove deep into the anatomy of unit economics and calculations.
- We answered key business questions with unit economic data.
- We explored the obstacles and benefits of time tracking.
- We unlocked the recurring revenue business model and the key metrics to manage.

Thank you for giving me the opportunity to be a guide. Unit economics is an elephant of an effort to grasp, but it's an important area to tackle. You're ready.

ABOUT STRIDE

stride

Stride Services was founded over 15 years ago and provides timely, accurate, and actionable outsourced bookkeeping and accounting services for high growth professional service firms around the United States. Stride's services incorporate automation and data analytics to unlock efficiency and actionable insights to drive growth and profitability for its clients.

Stride knows first-hand the challenges that service business owners have with finance. Our purpose at Stride is to support people with a thirst for learning to achieve their highest and best use by grounding stories with facts. We care deeply about helping entrepreneurs get and stay in their zone of genius and we believe that providing data to make smarter decisions will help them achieve the freedom they desire as a business owner. To learn more about Stride, you can check us out at www.stride.services or get in touch with me directly at russell.benaroya@stride.services.

ABOUT THE AUTHOR

Russell began his career on Wall Street after graduating from UC Santa Barbara with dual degrees in accounting and economics. After shifting his focus to entrepreneurship, Russell went on to receive his MBA from the Anderson School of Management at UCLA.

He has spent the last twenty years investing in private equity and as a healthcare entrepreneur, building and exiting two start-ups. In addition, he is a former Techstars graduate and a long-time member of EO (The Entrepreneurs' Organization).

Russell's genius zone is helping business owners achieve financial freedom. He is an experienced and strategic coach to entrepreneurs around all things finance. He shares his knowledge with both individual clients and groups, and previously taught a course on healthcare entrepreneurship at the University of Washington's Foster School of Business.

As a co-founder at Stride, Russell is responsible for engaging business owners to identify and help solve their back-office challenges. When he's not working on Stride, you can find him striding in the mountains pursuing his passion as an ultra distance trail runner. Russell currently is living in Seattle but wants to live in Costa Rica!

ACKNOWLEDGEMENTS

Special thanks to the team at Stride for caring deeply about the clients you serve. Every day, you work tirelessly to deliver on our service promise and get and stay in sync. I also want to honor the team for committing to and living our core principles that define how we want to be with each other and with our customers. These are:

- Harness the Wisdom of the Group
- Make and Honor Commitments
- Invest in Ourselves and Each Other
- Empowerment Works
- Practice Empathy
- Embrace Reality and Deal With It
- Use the 6 Step Process
- It's OK to Make Mistakes, Unacceptable not to Learn from Them
- Get and Stay in Sync
- Hire Well and Continually Train People
- Be Relentless about Creating an Impossibly Perfect Machine
- Optimize for Goals not Tasks or Functions

I also want to thank our clients for believing in what it means to have a true partner and working together to create a win for all. This book would not have been possible without the support of the Entrepreneurs' Organizations in Seattle, San Francisco, and Orange

County, all of which invited me to come and share my thoughts on unit economics with their members. And special thanks to Bailey Lang for helping me edit this and get it out the door.

Made in the USA
Las Vegas, NV
23 March 2026

44121508R00046